Growing Pains

Hannah Robinson

BookLeaf
Publishing

India | USA | UK

Presentation by *BookLeaf Publishing*

Web: www.bookleafpub.com

E-mail: info@bookleafpub.com

ISBN: 9789360942540

First edition 2024

From Pane to Pain

I view my life like panes of glass,
some clear, some stained,
each reflecting a piece of who I used to be.

With every year, my perspective shifts
from pane to pain,
trading frames of light
for shattered glass rimmed red,
matching the scars on my palms.

I view my life like panes of glass;
imperfect memories reflected in window frames
warped with age, peer back.

Sometimes I can see the edges of my memory
like surviving grains of sand
giving my life texture and grit,
something to hold on to
as life shifts ever forward.

With every year, my perspective shifts,
another year of my history
preserved in everlasting glass,
marking the end of yet another chapter.

Glancing back through my memory,
I find peace within my story,
for I know, after I'm gone,
the colors of my stained glass soul
will shine with reverie.

Perceptions Reflection

In a world hell bent
on breaking into factions,
where no one listens
or remembers how to grow,
we lose sight of our humanity.

Born into ancestral tunnel vision,
we're blinded by ignorance
before our newborn eyes can adjust to the light.
Never recognizing our blindness
until the shroud is ripped away.

As we blink into the light,
unfamiliar hands offer us back our sight.

Through these panes covering my eyes,
I witness the gradience of the world
reflected within its prism.

Through these reborn eyes,
I recognize there is no black and white.
When so many shades also catch the light,

there is only a spectrum
needing the touch of gentle hands
to set the world alight.

Tributary

3

I always find God on the water
where grace hangs pearl-gray in the dawn;
this river is an altar and I your spiritual allotter.

I always find God on the water.
He bids me to be a good daughter.
I baptize your ashes and watch until all signs of you are gone.

I always find God on the water
where grace hangs pearl-gray in the dawn.

Wild Hearts

Polite smiles and averted eyes
have become my currency
in a system where emotional honesty
has become something to demonize.

Day to day, I keep this mask in place,
stretching skin over broken glass teeth,
hiding all my fear, anxiety and grief beneath
as strangers admire their reflections
in the mirror of my face.

When does the flesh get to reflect the soul?
When may I also lose control?

If the Earth can crack and burst into flame,
why can I not do the same?

We live within her scars,
make room for her fury,
yet we're expected to live demurely
and forget we live behind invisible bars.

I yearn to be more like the Earth,
lying dormant in my peace
until I unleash and swallow the world with caprice
just to experience that freedom, and all its worth.

And so, I will forgo all polite decency,
diminishing in its friendly frequency.

Denying my smile for the use of public vanity
and descend into most immoral insanity.

Thy Cup Runneth Over

What is the purpose of a missing piece?
I've spent my life searching,
looking everywhere and within everyone.

Hoping to find irrefutable proof
that I'm not broken,
but incomplete.

Staring into the open eyes of lovers and strangers,
I find nothing but an abyss.

But within that darkness lies clarity.
There's nothing missing from within me.

I'm not a vessel waiting to be filled,
but an overflowing cup
taught to fear my own depth.

In truth, there are no gaps in my soul,
but bridges between my corner pieces;

love and respect,
faith and forgiveness,
grace and compassion.

The building blocks of my soul
have never known the touch of man,
nor shall they ever be defined by one.

Holy Wild

In the quiet, aching loneliness of nature,
I find my place in the universe.

Standing in the shade of ancient trees
whose leaves scrap the sky,
dwarfed in their size,
is like standing at the feet of God.

A cool breeze brushes my cheek
like a tender caress,
inviting me to linger there
in the silence of the holy wild

to teach me anew how to listen
for the sounds our modern world drowns out.

The Earth sings in spring's tender key,
whispering praise into the breeze
as flowers bloom and fade beneath my feet.

Such hauntingly beautiful melodies ring
in the dancing shadows of leaves.
Errant sunlight speckles my skin with gold,
adorning me like an altar.

Then the wind shifts,
and I am cast back
into heart-wrenching, sinful silence.

The March of Familiar Strangers

I catch glimpses of strangers wearing my face,
winking back at me before vanishing.

All my life these familiar strangers trail close behind,
some even being so bold as to walk beside me
wearing my smile with twice the shine.

These strangers never utter a word,
and yet I hear them speak.

Through daring stares and shoulders squared,
they part the seas of humanity with each stride;
looping their arms with mine,
they mark our steps in time.

A rhythm, steady as a heartbeat,
measured in its rise,
as new possibilities step into the light.

These familiar strangers I've known all my life
walk beside me with pride, before vanishing from
sight,
leaving me to take their place;
I find myself truly alive.

Transparent Soul

If my eyes are windows to my soul,
then my skin must be made of glass;
flitting unseen past the careless whole.

If my eyes are windows to my soul,
then give me those which are droll,
for I must laugh at the gazes that pass.

If my eyes are windows to my soul,
then my skin must be made of glass.

Murmurs of the Enigmatic Spirit

In my reflection, I see no one I know;
a specter peers back.
A haunting stranger with apathetic eyes
reflecting light but never feeling its warmth.

A specter peers back
It regards me with curiosity as the sun hits its face,
reflecting light but never feeling its warmth,
yearning to slip free from skin ice-cold.

It regards me with curiosity as the sun hits its face
eyes blazing with a fervent flame,
yearning to slip free from skin ice-cold.
They reach out, planting desperate palms against frigid glass.

Eyes blazing with a fervent flame,
a haunting specter peers back at me;
they reach out, planting desperate palms against frigid glass.
In my reflection, I see no one I know.

Holding Onto Time

As the years march by like proud soldiers
toward an uncertain future,
I feel the pull of the void,
plucking my earthly tether
to the rhythm of my heartbeat.

I remember my grandmother
buried alive in mementos from her youth,
fragments of her life she could grasp
until her knuckles bled white
as she held onto time.

The unyielding passage of time rolls on
like a ball of yarn, unspooling
until we reach the end of our thread.

As the years march by,
I find myself afraid to die,
having lost my sense of immortality
somewhere in my youth.

I cherish each moment,
reluctant to let any pass me by,
as I do my best to hold on to my remaining time.

Echoes Of Life In The Cosmos

Beneath a map of constellations,
I chart the course of my history,
honoring the truth built into its foundations.

Beneath a map of constellations,
I recall every tender sensation
and all the past's uncovered mysteries.

Beneath a map of constellations,
I chart the course of my history.

Growing Pains

To live is to evolve,
an existence dictated by change
and directed with new knowledge.

We are forever changing
our shape, our language,
our understanding of the world.

Every year, learning the box we lived within
can no longer shelter our fragile worldviews.

It hurts to change.

To sacrifice wide-eyed innocence
for adolescent knowledge still maturing,
hardly seems a fair transaction.

Often we flail for control,
grabbing at spider webbed strands,
hoping they will stop the free-fall
and that all will remain as it was.

There are no constants in life
but the persistence of change
and the fleeting part we play in its game.

It hurts to change,
but we were born ready
to withstand the growing pains
and the blessings they brace us for.

The Space Between Breaths

In the space between breaths, I count my blessings.
Lingering in the tranquil pause of infinity,
I see my life unfolding.

With each inhale, another memory
of sun-kissed days, running with bare feet,
ringing with laughter, wild and free.

Every exhale, a release
of the shadows buried beneath.
Moments words could never hope to reach,
known only to tear-stained cheeks
and desperate prayers for relief.

In the space between breaths, I count my blessings,
for time is fleeting and indiscrete in its passing.
Within each sacred pause, I see life

In all its shades,
my lungs breathing life into a stained glass soul
uniquely burdened and blessed.

Fractal Burn

I remember him when it storms.
How the sky would change its composition,
molecules contracting and exploding,
to make way for him.

With fumbling hands, I close the curtains,
but the thin arms of his lightning
stretch through the gaps underneath,
illuminating the fortress of my bedroom
until they reach me.

It's been years since the last storm,
yet it still feels like the first time.

With every flash, I glimpse my reflection
peering back from the dark ocean of my mirror,
a frightened stranger from years past.

The glass rattles in the tremor of his thunder.
Hail pelts the window in a syncopated barrage
like petty insults as I try to camouflage my fear
with wonder, giving my eyes another reason to widen.

As I lie there with knuckles bleeding white,
I whisper into the open air,
"The rain is full of ghosts tonight."

A Fragile Burden

In truth, I know little of what it means to be true;
my self-perception proving just as shallow
and one-dimensional as my reflection.

How does it feel to be so blatantly honest?
Your every emotion playing across your face,
painting your skin as if you are a perpetual blank canvas.

I imagine honesty to be such a fragile burden,
easily cracked and chipped away at.

Such a burden I could never bear,
and so I smile, hiding my meaning
behind a mouth full of broken glass,
showing the world my teeth,
rather than revealing me.

And yet, I catch a reflection of green eyes
watching as you splinter,
finding wonder in the way you fracture and mend.

Each fissured line, seamed with gold,
is a testament to you.

Your fragile burden became your blessing,
an honest, happy life worthy of highlight
while I resign myself to hide within plain sight.

The End of Rose-Colored Dreams

In the dawn's early glow,
no light strikes through
our rose-colored window,
once pleasant in its warm hue.

You carry on, as you always do,
never noting our monochrome gloom
or that no matter how much we wish it to,
there is nothing we can do to make love bloom.

And so, in the quiet shade
of yet another monochromatic day,
we confront the truth we only delayed,
by relinquishing our claims and parting ways.

You, Dear Heart, deserve more than what I gave
and though this is the end of our rose-colored dreams,
it is your name my memory shall engrave
and hold only in the highest of esteems.

Still Waters

In this world, content to rush through life
like white water over stone,
I am still.

Life, in all its mysteries,
will pass at any speed it pleases,
so I sit and take in the scenery.

My soul rests like a reservoir,
smooth as glass on the surface
but ever churning beneath,
a dangerous duplicity I struggle to release.

My body craves to run,
to race through every milestone
until all that's left is an empty memory.
And so I float,

soaking in the warmth of the sun,
reflecting its radiance;
I am baptized.

Love Like Prayer

To think of you is tantamount to praying,
 and to love you, I know no higher worship.
 A truer devotion I'd have no hope of portraying.

To think of you is tantamount to praying,
a simple act I'm powerless against obeying
as you uncover passions I intend to earth up.

To think of you is tantamount to praying,
and to love you, I know no higher worship.

Foreigner In A Familiar Land

When home feels foreign,
too cumbersome to pronounce
or hold on my tongue,
then what has it become?

I was grown here,
feet planted in lush, rich soil
turned arid and barren.
This was the orchard of my youth.

Reaching for the light hidden
beneath dancing shadows,
I broke through.

Hidden within the rings of my years,
milkweed blooms and the sky,
a sapphire shade of blue,
floods with summer tears.

Walking these paths I've known all my life
summons no memory of where they lead.

Familiar faces appear as mere shadows
of who they used to be.
Bright eyes, vibrant as flames,
dim as they meet my gaze.

Familiar faces whittled into my memory
no longer recognize me.

I no longer speak their tongue,
a foreigner in name and practice,
as I visit this place I once called home.

Beasts and Beauty

Children dream of castles,
ethereal and radiant,
spires that scrape the sky
where royal flags fly.

Dreaming of kingdoms
where magic is fact
and logic, a fantasy.

Children dream of castles
where beasts reside,
swallowed by thorns,
where princesses are beautiful,
and princes are brave,
but it's all a disguise.

Beasts are drawn to beauty
like moths to a heavenly flame,
reaching for purity
with hands stained by years of sin.

Yearning for the happy ending
promised to slumbering children
with drool on their chins.

Beasts are drawn to beauty impulsively
climbing towers like heroes
risking their lives
to hold grace in their arms

Beauties and beasts dream of castles,
of the security of spires,
and the childish comfort of dreams.

In The Dream Garden

When I was young, I had these dreams
telling me I'm meant for bigger and better things.
They clung to me like burrs,
snagging in my hair and catching on my clothes,
pressing into the earth beneath my soles,
paving a path I hoped to find when I grew old.

And though my path still winds,
edged with clover and thyme,
I find my way back to the garden.

Sitting in the shadow of dogwood trees
with all of my underdog dreams,
I listen to the birds flitting in the canopy
beating their wings,
scattering new dreams in the breeze
to take root, creating an arbor baptistry.

In the garden, I plant my dreams
where they may grow unseen;
lovely lilacs lulling in the breeze,
blissful begonias basking in the sun,
each growing so close they appear as one.

When I was young, I had these dreams,
and now they live within me,
using my soul as a trellis
as we reach for the light.

9 789360 942540